I Can Do It!

by Angie Quantrell
Illustrated by Cathy Lollar

*Y*ou *did not choose Me, but I chose you and appointed you that you should go and bear fruit, and that your fruit should remain, that whatever you ask the Father in My name He may give you. These things I command you, that you love one another" (John 15:16–17).*

I dedicate this book to my parents, all four of them! Ron, Bonnie, Bill, and Carole, none better could God have given me. Thank you for your love and support!

Woman's Missionary Union®
Birmingham, AL 35283-0010

Woman's Missionary Union
P.O. Box 830010
Birmingham, AL 35283-0010

Illustrated by Cathy Lollar

Dewey Decimal Classification: CE
Subject Headings: Christian Missions—Chinese Language—Children's
Literature

Series: I Can
ISBN 1-56309-626-9
W038103 • 0503 • 5M

How to Use This Book

Read this book with your preschooler. Talk about what happens to Meiying and her family.

For younger preschoolers, read the simple sentences on the lefthand pages. Tell what is happening in your own words. Point out features in the pictures.

Read the story to older preschoolers, discussing what is happening as you read. Try reading the words in Chinese at the bottom of the lefthand pages. Point to the Chinese symbols on each page and remind your preschooler that this is how the Chinese write their words.

Talk about similar missions activities your family has been involved in. Encourage your child to think of other missions ideas for your family to enjoy.

Choose one of the suggested missions activities at the end of this book to do with your family. Enjoy building a lifetime habit of doing missions with your preschooler.

我可以學習認識宣教

I can learn about missions.

Nhor holl ye hock jap yeng sic suun gao.

"Today we will learn about China," said Mrs. Murphy.

"Yea," said Meiying. "My grandparents came from China a long time ago."

"I have heard your parents talk about China," replied Mrs. Murphy. "Churches send special workers to China. Do you know what the workers do?"

Meiying smiled. "Yes," she said, "they tell people about Jesus."

"You are right," said Mrs. Murphy. "You are learning so much!"

"I can learn about missions," said Meiying.

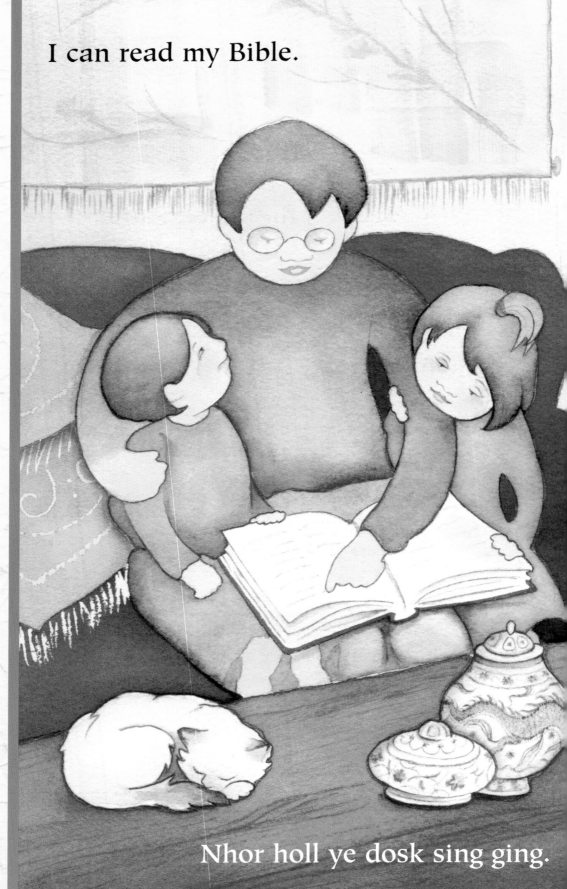

我
可
以
讀
聖
經

I can read my Bible.

Nhor holl ye dosk sing ging.

"Meiying," called her father, "come sit with me."

Meiying grabbed Fai and rushed to the couch. Meiying nestled on one side of her father, Fai on the other. Father smiled and said, "It is time to read our Bible, OK?"

Meiying and Fai grinned. They enjoyed spending time with their father. Father opened the Bible and read Meiying and Fai a story.

When they finished, Father said, "I am glad we have a Bible to read."

Meiying smiled. "Yes," she said. "I can read my Bible."

我可以讀聖經

5

I can give Bibles to others.

我可以贈送聖經給別人

Nhor holl ye jung sung sing ging cup beat yen.

Meiying watched a dragon dancing in the parade. "It's beautiful, isn't it Meiying?" said her father.

"Yes, Father," Meiying said. "It is exciting."

But Meiying was more excited about standing with her father beside a table piled high with Bibles. Some were in English, and some were in Chinese.

"Would you like a free book?" Meiying said to a young boy. "This book is about Jesus."

"Oh, thank you," said the boy. He took the Bible and walked away.

"We are sharing the story of Jesus," her father said.

Meiying's face had a big smile. "I can give Bibles to others."

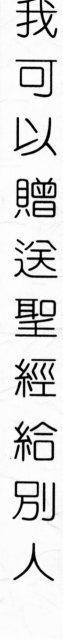

我可以贈送聖經給別人

7

I can go to church.

我可以上教會

Nhor holl ye shern gao wui.

"We're here, we're here," sang Fai.

Meiying said, "Fai, you must be happy to come to church!"

The family walked into the church and sat on a bench. Mother asked Meiying, "Why do we come to church?"

"We come to learn about Jesus," said Meiying.

"What is another reason we come to church?" asked Father.

Meiying thought hard. "Oh, I know," she said. "We come to learn how to do missions."

Meiying's parents nodded.

"I can go to church," she said.

我可以邀請朋友上教會

I can invite others to church.

Nhor holl ye yeu quing pung yao shern gao wui.

Meiying saw other children playing. "Hi, I'm Meiying," she said to a little girl on the tire swing. "Can we play?"

The little girl smiled. The new friends played. When Meiying's mother called them, Meiying said, "Would you like to come to church?"

"Yes," shouted Meiying's new friend.

"Let's talk to my mom about it," Meiying answered.

As Meiying walked with her new friend, Meiying thought *I can invite others to church.*

我可以邀請朋友上教會

I can give
an offering.

我可以奉獻

Nhor holl ye fung hin.

"Wow," said Meiying as she buckled her seatbelt, "this money is heavy!"

"I want to hold it," said Fai.

Meiying leaned over to place the ornate savings bank on Fai's lap.

"Be careful, Fai," said Mother. "We have saved our change for a long time to fill that bank."

"Yes," agreed Father. "This money will help missionaries all over the world."

"Heavy," said Fai.

Meiying smiled at Fai. "We are taking the offering to church. I can give an offering," she said.

我可以奉獻

13

我可以與別人分享

I can give
to others.

Nhor holl ye yu beat yen fun herng.

14

"Whew," said Meiying as she pulled the heavy bag up the stairs.

"We have full sacks," replied Mother. "Meiying, do you want to put the food into the collection box?"

Meiying nodded. She placed boxes and cans of food into the big box. Meiying noticed a sign on the box. "What does this say?" she asked her mother.

"It says, *Give food for the hungry*," read Mother. "We are giving food for the hungry."

"Oh," replied Meiying, "I can give to others."

我可以與別人分享

I can be a friend.

我可以與別人交朋友

Nhor holl ye yu beat yen gao pung yao.

"Wheee," sang Meiying and Anthony as they rode their bicycles.

Suddenly, a squirrel dashed in front of Anthony. "Look out!" said Meiying.

"Oh no!" yelled Anthony as he crashed and fell on the ground.

"Anthony, are you all right?" asked Meiying.

"No," cried Anthony, "I hurt my knee. It's bleeding."

"Let me help you," said Meiying. "I'll get my father to come."

"I can be a friend," said Meiying as she ran to get her father.

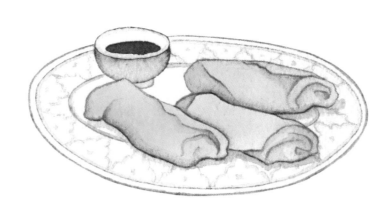

我可以與別人交朋友

我可以為朋友祈禱

I can pray for others.

Nhor holl ye wai pung yao kay toe.

Ring, ring rang the telephone. Meiying's mother answered it. After she hung up, she called the family.

"Meiying, your friend Meagan was in a car accident. She has a broken leg," said Mother.

"Will she be OK?" asked Meiying.

"She is going to be fine. We need to pray for her," answered Mother.

The family bowed their heads. "Dear Jesus, please help Meagan to get better, Amen," prayed Meiying.

"I can pray for others," said Meiying.

我可以為朋友祈禱

我可以幫助別人

I can help others.

Nhor holl ye bong zall beat yen.

Rip, crash went the bag. Meiying watched cans and groceries spill everywhere. An old man leaned on his cane, looking at the mess.

"Can we help him, Mommy?" Meiying asked.

"Great idea," said her mother with a smile.

Meiying picked up cans. She put them in a new paper sack.

"Here you go," said Mother, handing the man his sack.

"Thank you," he said.

He shook Meiying's hand. "Thank you, young lady," he said.

Meiying watched him walk away. "I can help others," she said.

我可以愛別人

I can love others.

Nhor holl ye.

The old woman swung her purse at the calico cat. "Get out of here!" she yelled.

Meiying watched the cat race over a fence. She looked at the woman's scowling face.

"Good afternoon," her father said to the woman.

"Hello," said Meiying.

"Humph," snorted the woman. She turned and stomped away.

Meiying's father smiled at her. "People have hard days, but Jesus says we should still love them," he said. "You were nice to her."

"Thank you," Meiying answered. "I can love others."

I can tell others about Jesus.

我
可
以
向
人
傳
講
耶
穌

Nhor holl ye hern yen chun kong yeh so.

"Brrroom," said Meiying as she drove her toy car on the track of the car mat.

"Park your car here," said Kim.

"Thanks," said Meiying, "but I am driving to church. It's over here."

"You always talk about church," said Kim.

"I like to go to church," said Meiying. "I can learn about Jesus."

"Jesus?" asked Kim. "Who is He?"

"Jesus is God's Son," said Meiying. "Jesus loves me. Jesus loves you."

"He loves me?" asked Kim.

"Yes, He does," said Meiying.

"Let me drive my car to church, too," said Kim.

I can tell others about Jesus, thought Meiying.

我可以參與宣教

I can do missions.

Nhor holl ye charm yu suun gao.

"I'm so excited," shouted Meiying. "I can't wait to help!"

"I can help too," said Fai.

"Meiying, you stand here, and serve the egg rolls," instructed Mother. "Fai, you stand by the fruit basket. Help people choose fruit."

"I'm glad our family is able to help serve this meal together," said Father.

"It is nice to serve a Chinese meal to others," said Mother.

Meiying used tongs to place an egg roll on a paper plate. She grinned at her father. "I can do missions! I can do it!"

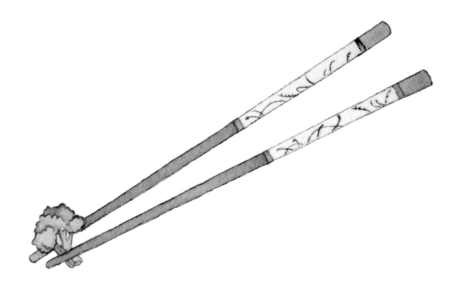

我可以參與宣教

27

A Note for Parents

This book is designed to teach parents and preschoolers about the importance of living a missions-minded lifestyle. Participating in missions activities as a family is a wonderful way to model being on mission for God. As preschoolers watch and help the family serve others in a variety of ways, they will internalize the mission of Jesus Christ. Daily, they will practice helping others, loving others, giving to others, doing for others, and telling others about Jesus.

As a family, choose simple missions activities that can be performed with all family members being involved. Ask preschoolers and children for their ideas about missions, and plan to participate in their ideas. Solicit ideas from missions teachers or magazines, selecting ones that will work for your family, or ones that you can adjust to fit your family's needs.

As you enjoy missions activities, use the words *missions* and *on mission with God.* Let your family see that being on mission with God is not scary, but important, fun, and a normal part of a healthy Christian lifestyle. Talk about missions in ways that your preschooler can understand. Let family members know that even performing simple missions activities is doing missions.

Enjoy missions. Let serving and helping others be your guide. Model the life of Christ and His mission.

Bible Thoughts to Use with Preschoolers

I was glad when they said, "Let us go to church" (see Psalm 122:1).
Bring an offering to church (see Mal. 3:10).
Help one another (see Gal. 5:13).
All that the Bible says is from God (see 2 Tim. 3:16).
Pray for one another (see James 5:16).
Love one another (see 1 John 4:7).

Read More About It

(For Parents)
To learn more about missions, read the following verses in the Bible. Memorize these verses and use them in your everyday activities.
Psalm 119:10–16
Mark 6:33–34
Mark 16:15–16
John 15:11–17
1 Corinthians 3:9,11
2 Corinthians 9:6–10
1 Thessalonians 1:2–4
1 Thessalonians 4:9–12
Titus 3:14

Missions Activities

Free Water. Materials: disposable cups; labels printed with the words *Jesus loves you!;* cooler filled with clean ice water; table

Choose a busy area in a local park or at an athletic event, and ask permission to give out free drinks of water. Set up a table with the cooler and cups. Place labels on cups and fill with cool water. Offer drinks to people passing by. Allow preschoolers and family members to help pass out water.

Adopt-A-Country. As a family, adopt a country as a study and prayer project. After locating your country on a globe, learn about it from maps, encyclopedias, books, and magazines. Display a map of your chosen country in a family meeting area. Prepare a meal with foods from your country, or do a craft project similar to the things people in your country do. Lead family members to pray daily for the unsaved people in your chosen country, as well as the Christian workers and missionaries who live there. Enjoy learning more about your adopted country.

Spare Change Jar. Materials: clean, empty jar; cutting magazines; glue; child-safe scissors

Guide family members to cut out faces of people from magazines. Glue faces to the jar, covering the entire jar. Encourage family members to place spare change in the jar. Or sacrifice a family outing or special meal, and place the saved money in the jar. Each time you place money in the jar, look at the faces on the jar, and lead family members in sentence prayers for lost people around the world. When the jar is full, donate it to a missions offering for the lost people of the world.

Verse-A-Week. Help your family learn a Bible verse a week. Begin by choosing a verse that encourages a missions lifestyle. Allow older preschoolers and children to copy the verse onto index cards. Give each family member a card, and post several around the house. Help younger preschoolers memorize the verse. Practice verses daily during dinner or other meals. Place learned verses in a box, and occasionally review them. Enjoy learning, applying, and hiding the Word of God in your family's heart.